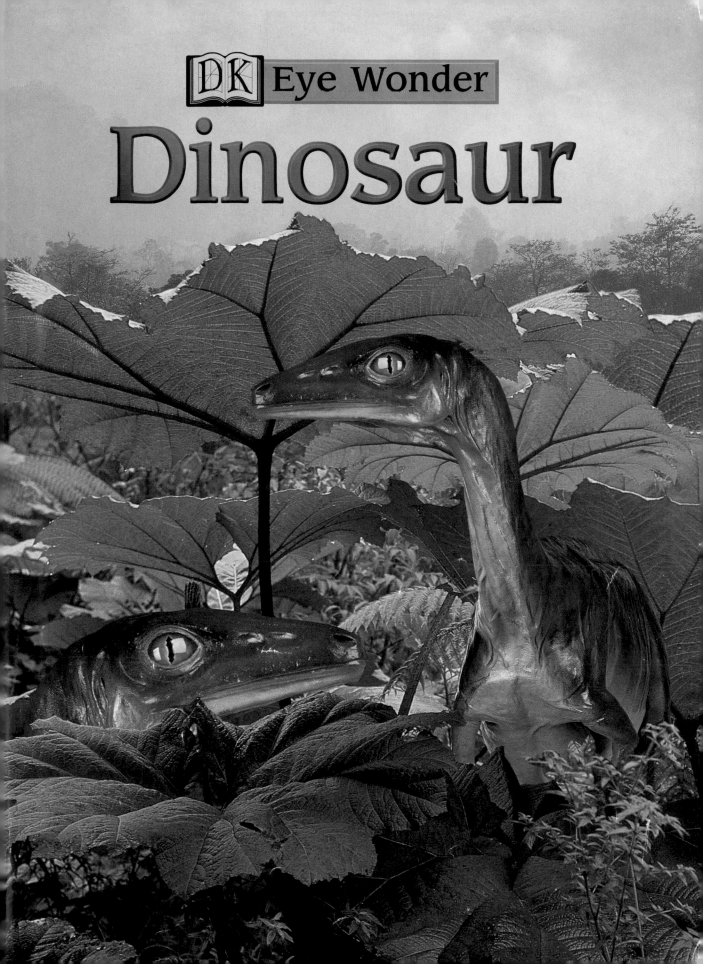

# DK Eye Wonder

# Dinosaur

LONDON, NEW YORK, SYDNEY, DELHI, PARIS, MUNICH, and JOHANNESBURG

**Written and edited by** Sarah Walker
and Samantha Gray
**Designed by** Janet Allis

**Publishing manager** Mary Ling
**Managing art editor** Rachael Foster
**US editors** Gary Werner and Magaret Parrish
**Jacket design** Chris Drew
**Picture researcher** Jo Haddon
**Production** Kate Oliver
**DTP Designer** Almudena Díaz
**Consultant** David Lambert

First American Edition, 2001

01 02 03 04 05 10 9 8 7 6 5 4 3 2 1

Published in the United States by
DK Publishing, Inc.
95 Madison Avenue
New York, New York 10016

Library of Congress Cataloging-in-Publication Data

Gray, Samantha
Dinosaurs / by Samantha Gray and Sarah Walker -- 1st American ed.
p. cm -- (Eye wonder)
ISBN 0-7894-7851-X -- ISBN 0-7894-8179-0 (lib.bdg.)
I. Dinosaurs--Juvenile literature. [I. Dinosaurs.] I. Walker, Sarah.
II. Title. III. Series
QE861.5 .G76 2001
567.9--dc21  2001017278

Color reproduction by Colourscan, Singapore
Printed and bound in Italy by L.E.G.O.

see our complete
catalog at
**www.dk.com**

# Contents

# What is a dinosaur?

Dinosaurs roamed the Earth for over 150 million years, then mysteriously died out. These reptiles varied from fierce killers to gentle plant eaters. Lifelike models help us to imagine what they looked like.

### Lizard legs

Like modern reptiles, most dinosaurs had scaly skin, a long tail, teeth, and claws. Today's reptiles have legs that splay sideways. Dinosaurs had straight legs directly below their bodies.

*Sharp teeth lined the powerful jaws of many meat-eating dinosaurs.*

*Short arms were used for grasping prey.*

### Feathered friends

It is likely that not all dinosaurs died out 65 million years ago. Some small, feathered dinosaurs may have survived. Today's birds probably descend from them.

*Birds have feet like those of many dinosaurs.*

### Motherly love

Clues to how dinosaurs behaved come from today's reptiles. Crocodiles are survivors from prehistoric times. They feed their babies and protect them. Some dinosaurs probably did this, too.

# Creature features

Dinosaurs had different features to equip
them for survival. Meat-eating dinosaurs
had sharp teeth and claws for hunting.
Some plant eaters grew to vast sizes.
Others had natural weapons such as horns.

*Some dinosaurs had
a row of spines along
their backs, from
head to tail.*

*Large tail helped
dinosaurs to
balance as they
leaned forward.*

*Most dinosaurs had
bumpy, scaly skin.*

*Muscular hind legs
allowed meat eaters
to chase their prey.*

## Dinosaur facts

● Dinosaurs were the biggest
land animals of all time,
although some whales, such
as the blue whale, are larger.

● Flying reptiles lived at the
same time as the dinosaurs,
but no dinosaur could fly.

● There were prehistoric
swimming reptiles, but no
dinosaurs swam in the sea.

# Dinosaur times

The age of the dinosaurs is known as the Mesozoic era. This stretched from 248 to 65 million years ago. It divides into three separate time spans: the Triassic, the Jurassic, and the Cretaceous.

*The Triassic period lasted from 248 to 206 million years ago.*

## Triassic world

At the start of the Mesozoic era, the continents were joined together into one supercontinent – Pangaea. This was surrounded by a massive ocean called Panthalassa.

## Jurassic world

Over millions of years, Pangaea split into two continents, Gondwana and Laurasia. As these drifted apart, different groups of dinosaurs evolved on each continent.

## Small beginnings

The Triassic world saw the first small dinosaurs. Like most early dinosaurs, meat-eating *Herrerasaurus* (he-rair-a-sore-us) walked on its hind legs.

*The Jurassic period lasted from 206 to 44 million years ago.*

*The Cretaceous period lasted from 144 to 65 million years ago.*

## Cretaceous world

The continents continued to drift apart and Earth began to look like it does today. The vast mountain ranges of the Andes and the Rockies were formed.

## and of the giants

ate in the Jurassic period, ant sauropods roamed in uge conifer forests, while *egosaurus* (steg-oh-sore-) ate low-growing plants. *hythyosaurs* (ick-thee-oh-re-us) swam in the seas.

## Dinosaur heyday

The great variety of Cretaceous dinosaurs included horned plant eaters like *Pentaceratops* (pen-ta-serra-tops) and huge meat eaters such as *Tyrannosaurus Rex* (tie-ran-o-sore-us recks).

# Skeletons

A skeleton tells a story. Teeth or bony beaks give information about what dinosaurs probably ate. Features such as horns show how they defended themselves. Small braincases tell us which dinosaurs had small brains!

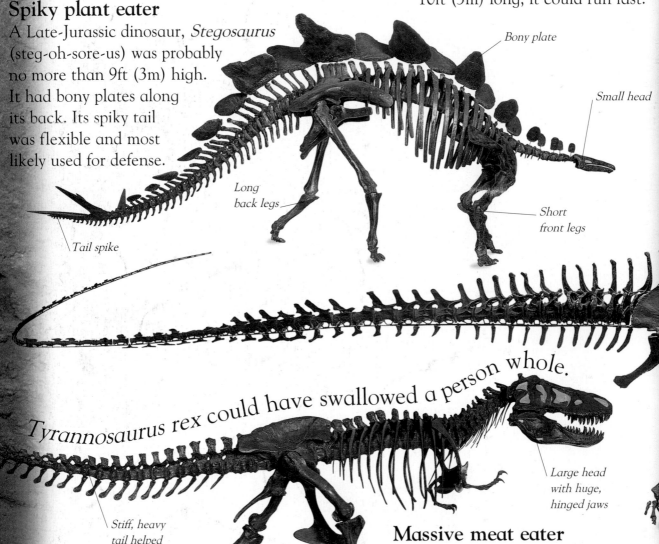

*Narrow jaw with sharp teeth*

## Small sprinter

A fossilized skeleton shows that *Coelophysis* (see-low-fye-sis) had long legs for its small size. Only 10ft (3m) long, it could run fast.

## Spiky plant eater

A Late-Jurassic dinosaur, *Stegosaurus* (steg-oh-sore-us) was probably no more than 9ft (3m) high. It had bony plates along its back. Its spiky tail was flexible and most likely used for defense.

*Bony plate*

*Small head*

*Long back legs*

*Short front legs*

*Tail spike*

*Tyrannosaurus rex could have swallowed a person whole.*

*Stiff, heavy tail helped balance*

*Powerful hind legs*

*Large head with huge, hinged jaws*

## Massive meat eater

Meat eaters like *Tyrannosaurus rex* (tie-ran-oh-sore-us recks) had massive jaws. They could open these extra wide to swallow large mouthfuls of flesh.

Long neck

Small head

Tail helped balance
while leaning
forward to sprint

Short arms

Long, strong
legs for running
at high speed

## Birdlike dinosaur

A fossilized skeleton of *Struthiomimus*
(strooth-ee-oh-meem-us) shows that it
had features in common with today's
ostrich. These include a small head
with a narrow beak, a long neck, and
powerful hind limbs.

## Jurassic giant

The longest of all the dinosaurs, sauropods like
*Diplodocus* (di-plod-o-kus) had small skulls containing
small brains! Despite its length, *Diplodocus* weighed
no more than two large elephants.

From head to tail, vast *Diplodocus* measured about 90ft (27.2m).

The sauropod's
skull is tiny
compared
to its body.

Long, stiff neck

## Horned head

The Late Cretaceous *Triceratops* (try-serra-tops)
was hunted by *Tyrannosaurus rex*. It probably
used its horns to defend itself. A plant eater,
it had a tough, toothless beak.

Bony frill

Brow
horn

Nose horn

Wide rib cage
supported
bulky body

Short,
sturdy legs

# Different dinosaurs

Dinosaurs are divided into two main groups, according to their hip bones. Some had hips arranged like a lizard's, and others had hips arranged like a bird's.

## Lizardlike

This group includes two-legged meat eaters such as *Tyrannosaurus rex* (tie-ran-oh-sore-us recks) as well as plant-eating sauropods like *Diplodocus* (di-plod-o-kus).

*Giant Saltasaurus (salt-tah-sore-us) lived in the Late Cretaceous period.*

## Bird bones

All bird-hipped dinosaurs were plant eaters. Some of the most familiar faces of the dinosaur world are found in this group!

*Iguanodon (ig-wahn-oh-don) lived in the Cretaceous period. It grew to 30ft (9.3m) long.*

## Dinosaur facts

● Strangely, experts think that today's birds evolved from lizard-hipped dinosaurs, not bird-hipped dinosaurs!

● To date, over 300 species of dinosaur have been found and named. Every few months more are discovered!

Tyrannosaurus rex *(tie-ran-oh-sore-us recks) lived in the Late Cretaceous period. It stood over 20ft (6m) tall.*

Galliminus *(gally-meem-us) lived in the Late Cretaceous period. It probably reached speeds of 43mph (70kph).*

Triceratops *(try-serra-tops) lived in the Cretaceous period. Its three sharp horns grew up to 3ft (90cm) long.*

Stegosaurus *(steg-oh-sore-us) lived in the Late Jurassic period. It had a toothless beak and a tiny brain!*

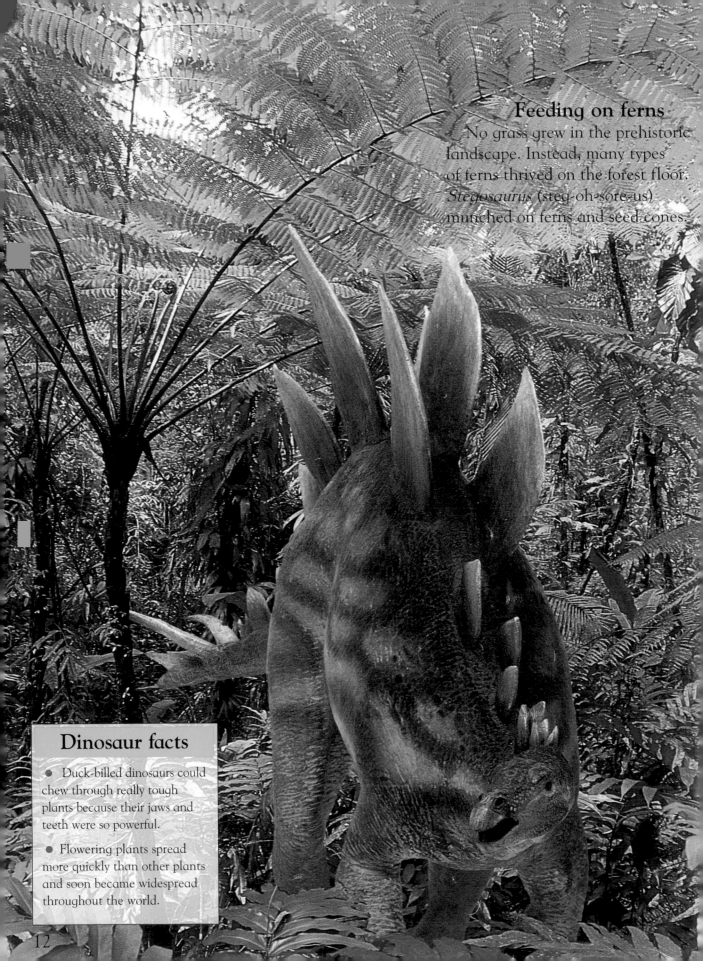

## Feeding on ferns

No grass grew in the prehistoric landscape. Instead, many types of ferns thrived on the forest floor. *Stegosaurus* (steg-oh-sore-us) munched on ferns and seed cones.

## Dinosaur facts

● Duck-billed dinosaurs could chew through really tough plants because their jaws and teeth were so powerful.

● Flowering plants spread more quickly than other plants and soon became widespread throughout the world.

# Dinosaur world

The dinosaurs' world was hot and
sunny, like today's tropics. There were areas
of desert, and forests of conifers and ferns.
Later, the first flowering plants appeared.

### Insect survivor

Some familiar insects
fluttered in prehistoric
skies. Modern dragonflies
look very much like this
fossilized dragonfly, which
lived 140 million years ago.

### Cycads

While dinosaurs ruled the
world, palmlike plants called
cycads were plentiful. They
still grow in some parts of
the world today, although
they are rare.

### Flower feast

Flowering plants, such as
magnolias, first appeared
in the Cretaceous period.
They were probably eaten
by plant-eating
dinosaurs.

### Prehistoric puzzle

Monkey puzzle trees thrived
on Earth long before the
dinosaurs. Today's monkey
puzzles are related to these.

### Mammal

One of the
first small mammals,
*Megazostrodon* (mega-zos-
troh-don) lived alongside early
dinosaurs. This furry model is
based on a tiny skeleton.

### Low life

Small meat eaters such as
*Compsognathus* (komp-sog-nay-
thus) hunted lizards and insects.
They ran fast, chasing their prey
through low-growing plants.

## Mighty meat eater

*Tyrannosaurus rex* (tie-ran-oh-sore-us recks) was one of the largest meat-eating dinosaurs. It would have been tall enough to peer into an upstairs window.

## Small but speedy

*Compsognathus* (komp-sog-nay-thus) was the size of a turkey. It may have been small, but its long legs meant it was built for speed. It could sprint fast after prey.

# Little and large

Dinosaurs of many shapes and sizes roamed prehistoric Earth. They varied from small, birdlike dinosaurs to the most enormous creatures ever to live on land. Largest of all were the giant, long-necked sauropods.

**Skyscraping sauropods**
Huge sauropods such as *Barosaurus* (barrow-sore-us) could nibble leaves from treetops as tall as a five-story building. They were so massive that nothing dared to attack a healthy adult.

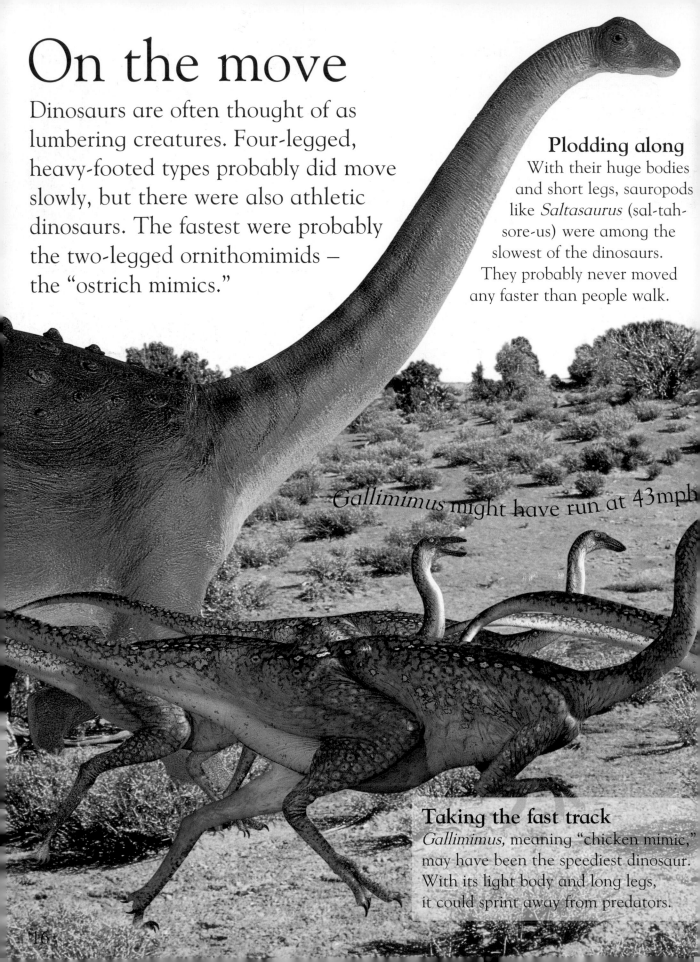

# On the move

Dinosaurs are often thought of as lumbering creatures. Four-legged, heavy-footed types probably did move slowly, but there were also athletic dinosaurs. The fastest were probably the two-legged ornithomimids – the "ostrich mimics."

**Plodding along**
With their huge bodies and short legs, sauropods like *Saltasaurus* (sal-tah-sore-us) were among the slowest of the dinosaurs. They probably never moved any faster than people walk.

*Gallimimus* might have run at 43mph

**Taking the fast track**
*Gallimimus*, meaning "chicken mimic," may have been the speediest dinosaur. With its light body and long legs, it could sprint away from predators.

## Fancy footwork

From footprints it is possible to see if a dinosaur was two-legged or four-legged. They also show whether a dinosaur was walking, trotting, or running.

## Road runners

Like ostriches, *Gallimimus* (gally-meem-us) had powerful legs for striding out. Unlike ostriches they had long tails, which helped them to keep their balance.

(70kph), which is faster than a winning racehorse.

### OOPS A DAISY!

It is not known if large, meat-eating dinosaurs could run fast. Their short arms could not break a fall if they lost their balance. An *Allosaurus* (allo-sore-us) found with 14 cracked ribs probably injured itself while running after prey.

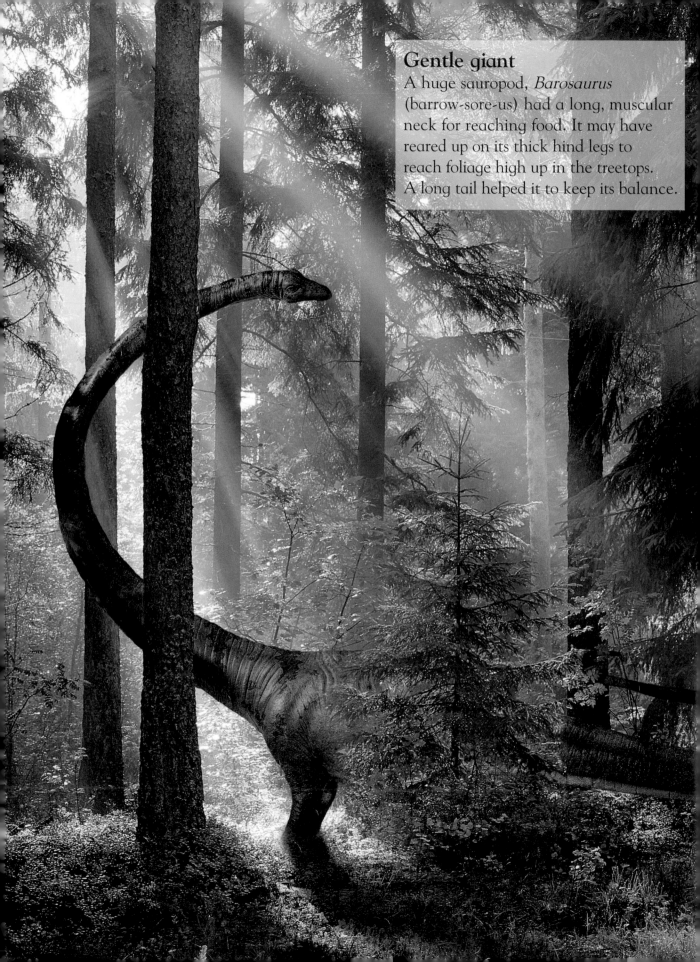

### Gentle giant
A huge sauropod, *Barosaurus*
(barrow-sore-us) had a long, muscular
neck for reaching food. It may have
reared up on its thick hind legs to
reach foliage high up in the treetops.
A long tail helped it to keep its balance.

# Plant eaters

Sauropods were the biggest plant eaters ever to walk the Earth. Most lived during the Jurassic period. Smaller plant-eating dinosaurs flourished before and after these giants existed.

Peglike teeth

## Tearing teeth

For stripping leafy twigs, *Diplodocus* (di-plod-o-kus) had teeth right at the front of its jaws. Perhaps this sauropod ate conifers, cycads, ferns, and tree ferns.

## Beak billed

*Hadrosaurs* (had-row-sores) had ducklike beaks for ripping up vegetation. They had more than 40 rows of teeth. They probably ate pine needles, seeds, twigs, and low leafy plants.

Strong teeth

Ducklike beak

### BOULDER EATERS

Sauropods such as *Apatosaurus* (a-pat-oh-sore-us) ate huge amounts of greenery each day to support their massive size. They did not chew the tough plants before swallowing. Instead they gulped down stones that ground up the food in their stomachs!

## Ground grazer

While sauropods munched treetop greenery, other dinosaurs tackled low-growing plants. *Edmontonia* (ed-mon-toe-nee-a) ate mainly ferns and mosses.

## Dinosaur facts

● Herd dinosaurs probably had excellent eyesight, hearing, and sense of smell to detect danger.

● Hadrosaurs are also known as duck-billed dinosaurs.

● Herds may have been noisy. Calls to each other probably warned of nearby predators.

## Forest friends

Giant herds of hadrosaurs, such as *Corythosaurus* (ko-rith-oh-sore-us), roamed through Cretaceous forests. They had hoofed fingertips for wading through swamps.

*Duck-billed dinosaurs could store food in their cheeks, like hamsters.*

# Hungry herds

Some plant-eating dinosaurs formed herds. There was safety in numbers, and they could warn each other of predators. They may also have traveled together to find food.

## Hiding in the crowd

Traveling as a herd makes it more difficult for predators to pick out just one animal. Today, as many as one million wildebeest herd together.

*Some hadrosaurs had head crests in weird and wonderful shapes.*

## Warning call

The hadrosaur *Parasaurolophus* (pa-ra-sore-oh-loaf-us) had a long, hollow head crest. It probably blew through this to make honking noises. In this way it could warn the rest of the herd of any danger.

## Horned defense

Herds could have used group defense tactics. *Triceratops* (try-serra-tops) may have formed a circle for protection, turning their horns outward to face an attacker.

## Following the tail in front

Some herds of plant-eating dinosaurs may have trudged vast distances to find good grazing land. Herds of *Pachyrhinosaurus* (pack-ee-rye-no-sore-us) may have walked from Canada to northern Alaska each spring to feed on large-leaved plants.

# Meat eaters

During the Cretaceous period, enormous, meat-eating dinosaurs ruled the land. Other creatures had to be on their guard against these ferocious hunters!

## King of the reptiles

*Tyrannosaurus rex* (tie-ran-oh-sore-us recks) was one of the biggest meat eaters ever to live on Earth.

## Dinosaur facts

● *Tyrannosaurus rex* had up to 60 teeth that were as long as knives, and just as sharp.

● The largest flesh-eating dinosaur was *Giganotosaurus* (jig-anno-toe-sore-us). This huge creature weighed an enormous eight tons!

# Pack hunte[r]

Some of the smaller, meat-eatin[g] dinosaurs snapped up prey such as small mammals, or eggs. Others pro[ba]ly ganged up in packs to overpower lar[ge] victims. Hunting in this way demand[ed] teamwork and intelligence.

*Sickle-shaped claw*

## Terrible talon

[V]elociraptor had a large, sharp claw [o]n the second toe of each hind foot. [H]eld off the ground for walking, the [cla]w could sweep out like a [swit]chblade knife [to sla]sh prey.

## Pack attack!

Savage hunters, *Velociraptor* (vell-oss-ee-rap[tor]) might have used group tactics to single out [and] attack victims. Raptors were well equipped to kill, with sharp claws, toothy jaws, an[d] agile bodies. These intelligent dinosa[urs] may have circled and ambushed t[heir] prey as lions do.

### Defend or die!

All was not over for *Protocera[tops]* (pro-toe-serra-tops). Its sharp beak was a useful weapon as it charged its enemy like a small rhinoceros.

## earsome fish eater

*uchomimus* (sue-koh-
ime-us) was an
normous, fish-eating
inosaur with a head like
crocodile's! It probably
vaded out into rivers and
akes to catch fish with its
aws or clawed hands.

*Long powerful jaws were
lined with more than
100 razor-sharp teeth.*

## Crocodile smile

Like *Suchomimus*, 
lived near water 
to snappy jaws,
curved claw f

## Scary skull

A relative of *Tyrannosaurus re*
*Albertosaurus* (al-bur-toe-sore-us)
was a frightening sight! It had
enormous curved teeth and could
move quickly after its prey.

*Flexible neck for swooping down on prey.*

## Present-day packs

Today's pack animals perhaps hunt in the same way as *Velociraptor*. In a wolf pack, some members herd while others lie in wait to ambush prey.

## Successful scavengers

*Coelophysis* (see-low-fye-siss) was a nimble, meat-eating dinosaur that lived and hunted in packs. They were not picky eaters and snapped up any creature they were able to swallow!

## Dinosaur facts

- It is likely that *Velociraptor* used its muscular legs to stamp on small prey, like secretary birds do today.
- *Coelophysis* had hollow bones and was a light, agile, and speedy predator.
- *Velociraptor* and *Protoceratops* both lived during the Cretaceous era.

# Tough tactics

Plant-eating dinosaurs were particularly at risk from predators. They needed protection from hungry meat eaters like this huge *Giganotosaurus* (jig-anno-toe-sore-us). Some had heavy coats of armor. Others made weapons of their claws, tails, or horns.

## Dinosaur facts

• Lots of the smaller dinosaurs did not have methods of defense. If attacked, they would simply run away!

• *Ankylosaurus* (an-kye-low-saw-rus) was covered in armor plating. Even its eyelids were protected! Only its underbelly was free from protection.

*Large, sharp teeth easily pierced the tough skin of victims.*

## Sharp thumb
*Iguanodon*
(ig-whan-oh-don)
was a peaceful plant
eater, but it
could use its
spiky thumb to
stab its enemy
if attacked.

## Terrible tails
*Euoplocephalus*
(yoo-op-loh-sef-ah-lus)
probably swung its hefty
tail club from side to side.

*A* Euoplocephales *tail club
was a dangerous weapon!*

## Whippy weapon
*Barosaurus* (bar-oh-sore-us)
may have used its long tail to
lash out at its enemies.

Barosaurus *could inflict a
stinging blow with its tail*

*Thin, bony plates
stuck up from*
Stegosaurus's *neck,
back, and tail.*

## Plated protection
*Stegosaurus*
(steg-oh-sore-us) was
a huge dinosaur about
the length of a truck!
To put off predators,
it had very tough skin
and pointed, bony plates.

## Dinosaur facts

● Living relatives of dinosaurs, such as birds and crocodiles, show how some dinosaurs may have been colored.

● The modern-day elephant is dull-colored in much the same way as large, plant-eating dinosaurs may have been.

*Markings break up an animal's outline so that they blend into the background.*

### Fading into forests
Large plant-eaters like *Iguanodon* (ig-whan-oh-don) probably had green scaly skin. Prowling predators would have found them hard to spot among the forest ferns!

# Camouflage

The coloring of dinosaurs is unknown, but there are clues from today's animals. Dinosaurs were probably colored and patterned for camouflage in their habitat.

*Did Velociraptor have green skin like iguanas?*

*... or pale skin with dark patches like leopards?*

*... or black stripes on reddish-yellow like tigers?*

## Lying in wait

Some meat-eating dinosaurs may also have had green or brown scaly skin. By blending into the background, they could sneak up on prey. See how this hunting crocodile looks like a log!

## Predator in disguise

*Velociraptor* (vell-oss-ee-rap-tor) most likely had a leopardlike coloring. A light, sandy skin would match its desert habitat while spots broke up its outline.

## Scaly story

Dinosaur scales did not overlap. They fitted together like floor tiles. Sometimes small scales surrounded larger ones.

*Scales may have been different colors to form a pattern.*

*Beadlike scales vary in size and shape.*

## Looking leafy

Today's lizards also have scaly skins. Like *Iguanodon*, this iguana lives in leafy surroundings. Its emerald-green scales hide it from predators in its rain forest home.

# Courtship

In the animal world, the strongest or most splendid-looking male has the best chance of attracting a female. Some dinosaurs may have challenged one another to trials of strength. Others showed off crests or frills.

*A thick bony dome crowned the top of the head.*

### Hard case
*Pachycephalosaurus* (pack-ee-seff-allo-sore-us), the "thick-headed lizard," had a dome of thick bone on top of its head. Maybe rival males head-butted or nodded to threaten each other.

Rival males may have shoved each other to show off their strength.

### Battle of the boneheads
In dinosaur herds, males faced a lot of competition to win a mate. The strongest males were most likely to be chosen to father young. *Pachycephalosaurus* males perhaps battled it out head to head.

## Fantastic frills

Male *Pentaceratops* (pen-ta-serra-tops) had larger frills than the females. These were decorative, and males probably showed them off to attract a mate or to frighten rival males.

## Spiky skull

The vast neck frill of the "spiked lizard" *Styracosaurus* (sty-rack-oh-sore-us) was fringed with six spikes. Males may have used these to impress females.

*Nose horn may have been used for jousting with rival males.*

## Colorful crests

*Corythosaurus* (ko-rith-oh-sore-us) had tall head crests. These were hollow and helped produce trumpeting calls. Males' tall crests may also have scared off rival males and impressed the females.

## Locking horns

Like some dinosaurs, some male mammals today seek to impress potential mates with displays of strength. Rams lock horns and try to push each other backward. The one losing ground finally slinks away from the winner.

# Nests and nurseries

Like most reptiles, dinosaurs laid eggs. Baby dinosaurs developed inside the egg. Some dinosaurs were caring parents. Others laid their eggs, then left their babies to fend for themselves.

## Eggs and nests

Lots of dinosaurs laid their eggs in nests. Some nests were simple pits dug into the earth, while others were built with mud. The egg shells were brittle like those of birds' eggs, so that baby dinosaurs could break through them to hatch.

## Parental protection

This *Oviraptor* (oh-vee-rap-tor) died wrapped around her nest. She may have been trying to protect her brood. It is likely that she was smothered by wet sand. This probably happened during a rainstorm more than 80 million years ago.

*Young* Leallynasaura *may have squawked to get their parents' attention!*

## Dinosaur facts

● *Maiasaura* (my-a-sore-a) means "good mother lizard." These gentle dinosaurs carefully looked after their babies when they were born.

● Some dinosaur eggs were tiny, yet the babies often grew into enormous creatures!

# Happy families

*Leaellynasaura* (lee-el-in-a-sore-a) may have nested together in big groups like some seabirds do today. There is safety in numbers! After the eggs hatched the parents probably looked after their babies for several months. It is likely they kept them warm and protected them from predators.

*Parents probably brought food for the baby dinosaurs*

# High flyers

While dinosaurs roamed the land, the skies were ruled by flying reptiles called pterosaurs. Large pterosaurs most likely flew over water, swooping down to catch fish. Smaller ones probably snapped up insects in the air.

**Giant of the sky**
The biggest flying animal that ever lived, *Quetzalcoatlus* (kwet-zal-koh-at-luss) may have weighed as much as a large human being. To support its weight, this Late-Cretaceous pterosaur had a wingspan like that of a light aircraft.

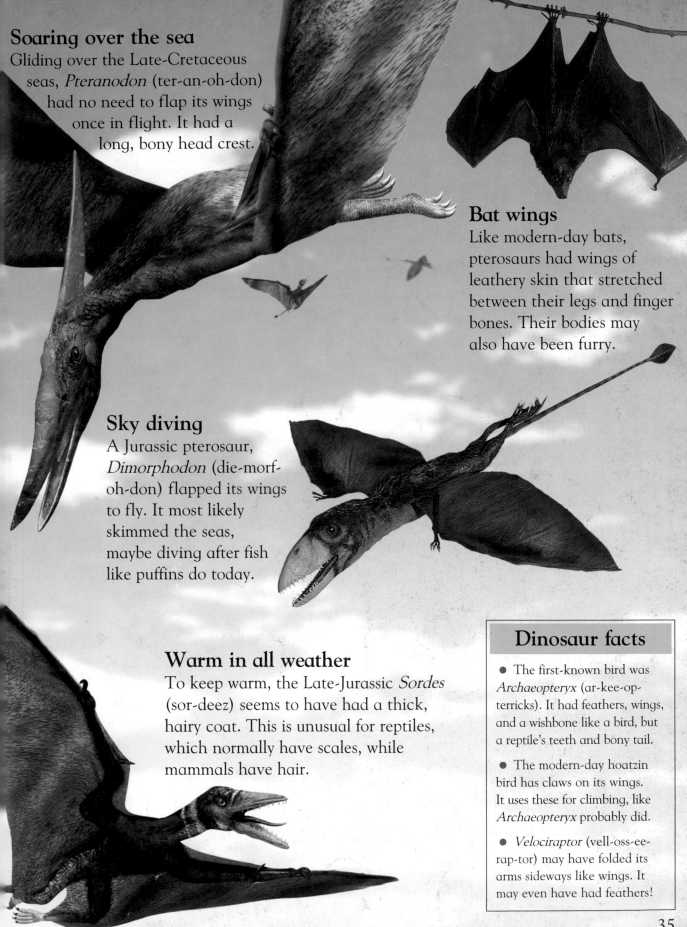

## Soaring over the sea
Gliding over the Late-Cretaceous seas, *Pteranodon* (ter-an-oh-don) had no need to flap its wings once in flight. It had a long, bony head crest.

## Bat wings
Like modern-day bats, pterosaurs had wings of leathery skin that stretched between their legs and finger bones. Their bodies may also have been furry.

## Sky diving
A Jurassic pterosaur, *Dimorphodon* (die-morf-oh-don) flapped its wings to fly. It most likely skimmed the seas, maybe diving after fish like puffins do today.

## Warm in all weather
To keep warm, the Late-Jurassic *Sordes* (sor-deez) seems to have had a thick, hairy coat. This is unusual for reptiles, which normally have scales, while mammals have hair.

### Dinosaur facts

● The first-known bird was *Archaeopteryx* (ar-kee-op-terricks). It had feathers, wings, and a wishbone like a bird, but a reptile's teeth and bony tail.

● The modern-day hoatzin bird has claws on its wings. It uses these for climbing, like *Archaeopteryx* probably did.

● *Velociraptor* (vell-oss-ee-rap-tor) may have folded its arms sideways like wings. It may even have had feathers!

# Under the waves

The world was much warmer when the dinosaurs lived, and there were no icebergs in the seas. No dinosaurs lived underwater, but prehistoric oceans brimmed with a variety of other weird and wonderful reptiles.

## Speedy swimmer
*Ichthyosaurus* (ick-thee-oh- sore-us) means "fish lizard." These reptiles looked like dolphins but swam like sharks, flicking their strong tails from side to side. They gave birth to live young underwater.

## Fearsome hunter
*Liopleurodon* (lie-oh-ploor-oh-don) had vast, powerful jaws that snapped shut on its unfortunate victims.

The enormous neck of *Elasmosaurus* grew up to 23ft (7m) long

## Shark survivors
Sharks have existed for millions of years. They have swum in the world's oceans before, during, and after the time of the dinosaurs.

## Giant sea serpent

*Elasmosaurus* (ee-laz-moe-sore-us) had two pairs of flippers. It flapped these like wings to glide through the water. Females probably came ashore to lay their eggs in the sand, risking dinosaur attacks.

### "NESSIE," THE LOCH NESS MONSTER

People claim to have seen a sea serpent swimming in Loch Ness in Scotland. "Nessie" is described as looking like an *Elasmosaurus*. Whatever killed the dinosaurs killed *Elasmosaurus* too, but Loch Ness is very deep. Some people believe that Nessie hides in the depths.

# Brain power

A simple way to measure intelligence is to compare the size of the brain to the size of the body. The brightest dinosaurs had bigger brains in relation to their body size than the less-intelligent dinosaurs.

*Small head housed a small brain.*

*Modern mammals like the tiger are near the top of the class for animal intelligence.*

## Dinosaur dunce

Sauropods were among the least intelligent of the dinosaurs. They had vast bodies but tiny heads, with space for only a small brain!

*Birds are next in intelligence to mammals.*

## Not so bright!

Dinosaurs most likely did not have the brain power of today's mammals and birds. Roaming Earth for millions of years, they still had enough brain power for successful survival.

*Dinosaurs were less intelligent than today's birds.*

*Modern reptiles are less intelligent than some of the small hunting dinosaurs were.*

# e dinosaurs

...saurs roamed
... ago. Yet
...but their
...ed out.
...uncertain.

...in the Gulf of Mexico
...roid hitting Earth.
...illion years ago, at
...inosaurs disappeared.
...the Earth's atmosphere,
...to the death of the dinosaurs.

The asteroid would have hit Earth at an

D...

● The ...
being, *Tr...*
eyes. Thes...
dusk, and s...

● *Troodon* ...
tooth." It prob...
it could slash w...
tear apart with i...

# Death of th

Hundreds of different dino
the Earth 75 million years
10 million years later, all
descendants the birds d
What happened is still

## Huge hollow
An enormous crater hidden
was caused by a giant aste
The impact occured 65 n
the same time that the
It dramatically change
and may well have le

inosaur facts
ize of a tall human
odon had very large
helped it to hunt at
ot small prey.
eans "piercing
ably ate anything
h its claws and
teeth.

## Deadly impact

The asteroid created a vast crater, similar to this one, when it hit Earth. Huge clouds of rock and dust blocked the Sun. These shielded out light and destroyed almost all plant life.

## Dinosaur facts

● Today's birds may have evolved from some of the small, feathered dinosaurs.

● An asteroid hitting Earth may not have caused the dinosaurs to die out instantly. This probably occurred as the climate began to change.

*When this dinosaur died, it was quickly buried under layers of mud and river sludge.*

## Survival of the toughest

Some animals lived through the changes in the Earth's atmosphere. Scorpions, turtles, birds, and insects were just some of the ones strong enough to survive!

*In time, the layers covering the dinosaur turn to rock. The bones become incredibly hard over millions of years.*

*The wind and rain wear away the rock. Scientists discover the dinosaur bones and begin removing them from their tomb.*

## Rare reward

Fossils are the remains of things that lived long ago. Dinosaur fossils are a rare find. They are usually found in rock layers that formed at the bottom of swamps, lakes, or rivers.

*Over a long period of time, movements deep within the Earth force the skeleton toward the surface.*

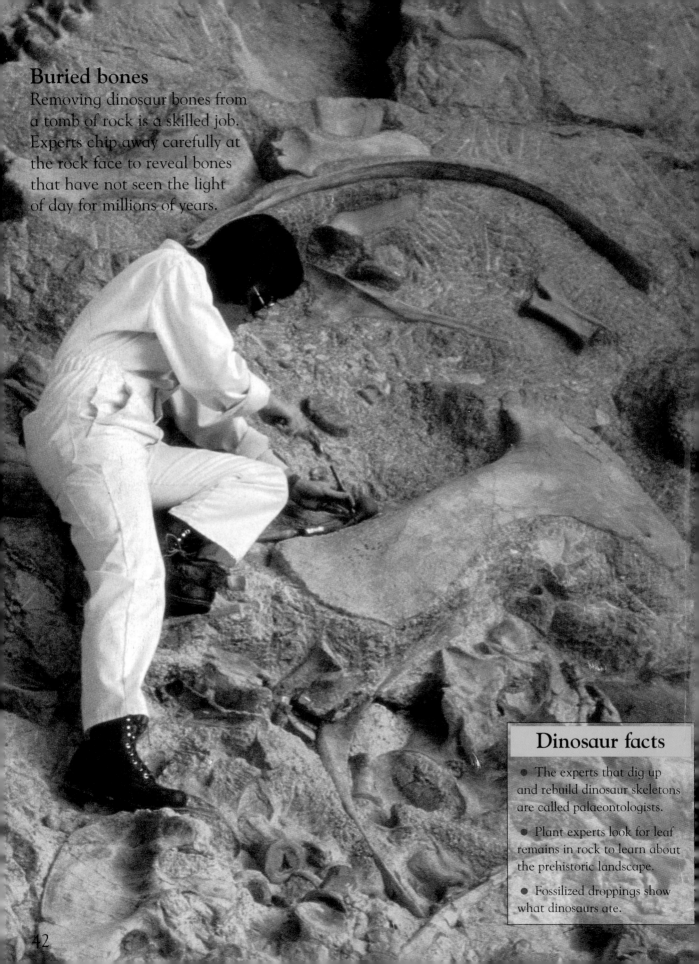

## Buried bones

Removing dinosaur bones from
a tomb of rock is a skilled job.
Experts chip away carefully at
the rock face to reveal bones
that have not seen the light
of day for millions of years.

### Dinosaur facts

● The experts that dig up
and rebuild dinosaur skeletons
are called palaeontologists.

● Plant experts look for leaf
remains in rock to learn about
the prehistoric landscape.

● Fossilized droppings show
what dinosaurs ate.

# Digging up dinosaurs

Fossilized dinosaur bones can lie hidden in ancient rock. Dinosaur detectives, called palaeontologists, search for buried fossils. Sometimes they find fossilized bones, teeth, and footprints. The most exciting finds are whole dinosaur skeletons.

### Plaster protection
Palaeontologists wrap bones in bandages and runny plaster. This sets hard, protecting the surface of the bone like plaster casts protect broken legs.

### Careful cleaning
The bones are taken to a museum where the plaster is cut away. They may even arrive still inside the rock. Cleaning the bones is a skilled job.

### Prehistoric puzzle
Rebuilding a prehistoric skeleton from a jumble of bones is a tricky task. It is like putting together a difficult jigsaw puzzle!

*Palaeontologists piece together a Pliosaurus skeleton.*

# Building dinosaurs

Rebuilding a dinosaur is a lengthy process. Fossilized bones are removed from ancient rock. Experts then make a copy of these. Getting the replica bones ready for display is very complicated and can take a long time!

## Making the mold

An expert begins by carefully painting each of the fossilized bones with liquid rubber. When the rubber dries, it makes a flexible mold.

## Putting it all together

The molds are removed from the bones and coated in liquid plastic. This forms the outside of the replica skeleton.

*Each limb bone is molded in two halves*

## Filling the bones!

Liquid plastic is poured inside the hollow molds. This sets into a stiff foam.

## Finishing touches

The outer molds are removed to reveal the replica bones. They are pieced together and painted to look like real bones. The replica skeleton is then displayed for everyone to see!

## Recreating the past

This lifesize copy of a *Barosaurus* (barrow-sore-us) skeleton is displayed in a New York museum. Metal rods are welded together to keep it in position. It is mounted on a supporting metal frame.

*Guide ropes keep the replica steady as it is moved into position.*

*This replica is over 49ft (15m) high. It towers over visitors to the museum!*

This *Barosaurus* is shown rearing up on its hind legs!

45

# Glossary

**asteroid**  A lump of rock that orbits the Sun.

**camouflage**  Camouflage is usually skin coloring that makes animals look the same as their surroundings. This is to avoid being seen by predators.

**carnivore**  An animal that eats the flesh of another animal.

**conifer**  An evergreen tree that produces seeds in cones.

**continent**  One of the Earth's great land masses.

**crater**  A hollow in the ground, as caused by an explosion or an object from space hitting Earth.

**Cretaceous**  The last period of the dinosaur age. It started about 140 million years ago and ended about 65 million years ago.

**cycad**  A stumpy plant similar to a palm tree. Cycads and cycadlike cycadeoids were very common during the dinosaur age.

**era**  A long stretch of prehistoric, or historic, time made up of periods.

**evolve**  All living things change over long periods of time. These changes occur gradually over generations, allowing creatures to adapt to their surroundings.

**extinction**  The death of a whole species.

**fossil**  The preserved remains of a creature or plant that was once alive.

**habitat**  The place where a creature or plant naturally lives or grows.

**Jurassic**  The middle period of the dinosaur age. It began about 200 million years ago and ended about 140 million years ago.

**mammal**  A warm-blooded animal with a hairy body and a backbone. Female mammals produce milk to feed their young.

**migration**  The regular, seasonal journey of animals from one place to another to find food, warmer weather or to breed.

**Mesozoic**  The age of the dinosaurs. This includes the Triassic, Jurassic and Cretaceous periods.

**paleontologists**  Experts that dig up and rebuild dinosaur skeletons.

**predator**  An animal that hunts another animal for food.

**prehistoric**  Belonging to a time before history was recorded in written form.

**prey**  Creatures that are hunted by other creatures for food.

**reptile**  A cold-blooded, egg-laying animal that is covered in scales.

**scale**  A small, thin plate that protects the skin of reptiles and fish.

**scavenger**  An animal that eats the remains of a creature that another animal has killed.

**species**  A group of animals or plants made up of related individuals who are able to produce young with one another.

**Triassic**  The first part of the dinosaur age. It lasted from about 245 to 200 million years ago. Dinosaurs evolved toward the end of the Triassic period.

# Animal alphabet

Every dinosaur and prehistoric creature featured in this book is listed here, along with its page number, its characteristics, and when it lived.

**Albertosaurus** 23
*A two-legged meat eater.*
*(Cretaceous)*

**Allosaurus** 17
*A two-legged meat eater.*
*(Jurassic)*

**Ankylosaurus** 26
*A four-legged plant eater.*
*(Cretaceous)*

**Apatosaurus** 19
*A four-legged plant eater.*
*(Jurassic)*

**Barosaurus** 15, 18, 27, 45
*A four-legged plant eater.*
*(Jurassic)*

**Baryonyx** 23
*A two-legged fish eater.*
*(Cretaceous)*

**Coelophysis** 8, 25
*A two-legged meat eater.*
*(Triassic)*

**Compsognathus** 13, 14
*A two-legged meat eater.*
*(Jurassic)*

**Corythosaurus** 20, 31
*A two-legged plant eater.*
*(Cretaceous)*

**Diplodocus** 9, 10, 19
*A four-legged plant eater.*
*(Jurassic)*

**Edmontonia** 19
*A four-legged plant eater.*
*(Cretaceous)*

**Euoplocephalus** 27
*A four-legged plant eater.*
*(Cretaceous)*

**Gallimimus** 11, 16-17
*A two-legged meat eater.*
*(Cretaceous)*

**Giganotosaurus** 22, 26
*A two-legged meat eater.*
*(Cretaceous)*

**Hadrosaurs** 19, 20-21
*Plant eaters that could walk on two legs or four.*
*(Cretaceous)*

**Herrerasaurus** 6
*A two-legged meat eater.*
*(Triassic)*

**Iguanodon** 10, 27-29
*A two-legged plant eater. It could run on two legs or walk on four.*
*(Cretaceous)*

**Leallynasaura** 32-33
*A two-legged plant eater.*
*(Cretaceous)*

**Maisaura** 32
*A two-legged plant eater.*
*(Cretaceous)*

**Oviraptor** 32
*A two-legged meat eater.*
*(Cretaceous)*

**Pachycephalosaurus** 30
*A two-legged plant eater.*
*(Cretaceous)*

**Pachyrhinosaurus** 21
*A four-legged plant eater.*
*(Cretaceous)*

**Parasaurolophus** 21
*A two-legged plant eater.*
*(Cretaceous)*

**Pentaceratops** 7, 31
*A four-legged plant eater.*
*(Cretaceous)*

**Protoceratops** 24-25
*A four-legged plant eater.*
*(Cretaceous)*

**Saltasaurus** 10, 16
*Four-legged plant eater.*
*(Cretaceous)*

**Sauropods** 7, 9, 15, 16, 18-19, 38
*Four-legged plant eaters.*
*(Jurassic, Cretaceous)*

**Stegosaurus** 7, 8, 11, 12, 27
*A four-legged plant eater.*
*(Jurassic)*

**Struthiomimus** 9
*A two-legged dinosaur. It ate both plants and meat.*
*(Cretaceous)*

**Styracosaurus** 31
*A four-legged plant eater.*
*(Cretaceous)*

**Suchomimus** 23
*A two-legged fish eater.*
*(Cretaceous)*

**Triceratops** 9, 11, 21
*A four-legged plant eater.*
*(Cretaceous)*

**Troodon** 39
*A two-legged meat eater.*
*(Cretaceous)*

**Tyrannosaurus rex** 7-11, 14, 22-23
*A two-legged meat eater.*
*(Cretaceous)*

**Velociraptor** 24-25, 29, 35
*A two-legged meat eater.*
*(Cretaceous)*

## Other animals

**Archaeopteryx** 35
*A prehistoric bird*
*(Jurassic)*

**Dimorphodon** 35
*A fish-eating flying reptile.*
*(Cretaceous)*

**Elasmosaurus** 36-37
*A fish-eating sea reptile.*
*(Jurassic)*

**Ichthyosaurus** 7, 36
*A meat-eating sea reptile.*
*(Jurassic)*

**Liopleurodon** 36
*A meat-eating sea reptile.*
*(Jurassic)*

**Megazostrodon** 13
*A tiny meat-eating mammal.*
*(Jurassic)*

**Pliosaurus** 43
*A fish-eating sea reptile.*
*(Jurassic)*

**Pteranodon** 35
*A fish-eating flying reptile.*
*(Cretaceous)*

**Pterosaurs** 34-35
*Flying reptiles that lived throughout the Mesozoic Era.*

**Quetzalcoatlus** 34
*A meat-eating flying reptile.*
*(Cretaceous)*

**Sordes** 35
*An insect-eating flying reptile.*
*(Jurassic)*

# Index

## Useful websites

www.enchantedLearning.com/subjects/dinosaurs/
*Everything you need to know. Lots of facts about all dinosaurs, plus quizzes, games, and printouts.*
http://www.bbc.co.uk/dinosaurs/
*Takes you on an interactive journey! Lots of fact files, games, and articles by experts.*

## Acknowledgments

**Dorling Kindersley would like to thank:**
Hilary Bird for preparing the index, Jon Hughes for digital illustrations, Andrew O'Brien for additional digital artwork p18, Clare Shedden and Mo Choy for design assistance, and Rachel Hilford for picture library services.

## Picture credits